A FOREVER FAMILY

Story and Pictures by **ROSLYN BANISH**
with **JENNIFER JORDAN-WONG**

 **HarperCollins***Publishers*

To Jennie Barr Epstein
—R.B.

To two very special
people,
Mom and Dad
****

A FOREVER FAMILY
Copyright © 1992 by Roslyn Banish
Printed in the U.S.A. All rights reserved.
1 2 3 4 5 6 7 8 9 10
First Edition

Library of Congress Cataloging-in-Publication Data
Banish, Roslyn, date
  A forever family / story and pictures by Roslyn Banish with
Jennifer Jordan-Wong.
      p.   cm.
  Summary: Eight-year-old Jennifer Jordan-Wong describes her
adoption by a family after four years of living as a foster child
with many different families.
  ISBN 0-06-021673-5. — ISBN 0-06-021674-3 (lib. bdg.)
  1. Jordan-Wong, Jennifer—Juvenile literature.   2. Children,
Adopted—United States—Biography—Juvenile literature.
[1. Adoption.   2. Foster home care.   3. Family life.   4. Jordan-
Wong, Jennifer.   5. Children's writings.]   I. Jordan-Wong,
Jennifer.   II. Title.
HV874.82.J87B36   1992b   90-28725
362.7′34′092—dc20   CIP
[B]   AC

My name is Jenny.

I am 8 years old.

Last year I was adopted.

This is my mom and dad.
They adopted me when I was 7.

I am in the second grade.

My favorite thing at school is relay races.

I can run fast.

There are other things I like to do.

I love to read Nancy Drew books.
I have already read 33 of them.
What will I do when I have read all of them?

I play the piano.

Every Monday I go to my piano teacher's house
for a lesson.

Here I am practicing.

That's my mom looking over my shoulder.

I also like to Hula Hoop.

The longest I have ever Hula Hooped is one minute.

And I like to bake chocolate-chip cookies
with my friend.
Her name is Jennie too, but she spells it
a different way.
Jennie and the other kids at school want to know,
"What is it like being adopted?"
Or they ask, "How come you're adopted?"

My biological parents—the parents I was born from—
loved me.
But they had lots of problems.
They couldn't take care of me.
That is why, when I was 3,
I had to go live with foster parents.
Foster parents take care of you
when your own parents can't.
Foster parents are usually temporary parents.
They take care of you until you are adopted.
But not everybody gets adopted.

This is Stephanie and Otis.

They were my second foster mom and dad.

I went to live with them when I was 6.

Before that, I lived with my first foster family.

It was hard to keep changing families.

The little boy is Baby Otis.
He is Stephanie and Otis's child.

Sometimes Baby Otis is fun to play with
and sometimes he is not.

Stephanie loves me and Otis loves me.

I love them too.

I like to go back and visit them.

This was my room at Stephanie and Otis's house.
I shared it with my foster sister.
She used to sleep on the top bunk
and I slept on the bottom.
Now Stephanie and Otis have other foster kids.

This is Anita and Marian.

They are social workers. Social workers help people.

They make sure that somebody
is taking good care of you.

If your parents can't take care of you, they find
foster parents or parents who want to adopt you.

When I was living with Stephanie and Otis,
I used to visit Anita and Marian in their office.
We talked a lot and became good friends.

My mom and dad talked to Anita and Marian
a lot too.
They talked about wanting to adopt a child.
Anita and Marian knew them very well.
They also knew me very well.
Anita and Marian thought we would be a good family.
So they introduced us to each other.

It was very scary meeting my new mom and dad.

But then we spent lots of weekends together.
Sometimes we went to the country.
We went swimming and picked blackberries
and rode bikes and got to know each other.

We knew we wanted to be a family.

They wanted to adopt me and I wanted to live
with them.

We would become a forever family.

There was a ceremony in a courtroom
for my adoption.
Lots of our friends and relatives came.
I was really nervous and excited.
Judge Hodge read some important papers out loud.

Then my mom and dad stood up in the courtroom
and said,
"We most earnestly desire to become
the adoptive parents of Jennifer....
We want to share our lives with her; we want to share
our experiences and wisdom with her.
We love Jennifer!"

The judge signed the papers.
Then he said I was officially adopted.
Now we were a forever family!

After the ceremony there was a party for me with lots of people who are important to me: Marian, Anita, my mom and dad, Vanessa, Judge Hodge, Nancy, Grandma, Grandpa, my cousins, my uncle Gene, and my friends.

I got some presents!

At first it was hard to call my parents
"Mom" and "Dad."
But it got easier.
Now they really feel like Mom and Dad.

And lots of other things were new and different too.
Like eating bagels and cream cheese.

And having my own room.

And having new grandparents.

Here are my dad's parents.

I call them "Grandma" and "Grandpa."

They love me a lot.

I love them, too.

Here I am looking at pictures of my grandparents
when they were younger...

黃蘭素

and this is me learning how to write
my name in Chinese.

All these people are my relatives.
It's Chinese New Year, and we're celebrating
three birthdays: mine, Grandpa's, and Aunt Ella's.

We had three
birthday cakes.
This is my Grandpa
blowing out the candles
on his cake.

And this is me
with my cake.

My other grandparents, my mom's parents, died before I got the chance to meet them. This is a picture of them my mom has.

Uncle Gene, my mom's brother, and Aunt Layton
have lots of kids.

Here I am with three of them: Rachel, Johanna,
and Alexa.

I visit my cousins every summer.

We do fun things together.

Sometimes they feel like sisters.

Alexa is the baby.

She's fun to play with, but I don't like it when she drools on me.

I wonder what I was like when I was a baby.

Aunt Layton says I was probably a lot like Alexa—
cute and smart and looking around all the time.
I know my biological mother could tell me
what I was really like.

I still think about her.

How come she couldn't take care of me?

Why did she have so many problems?

What is she doing?

Will I ever see her?

Is she okay?

I have lots of questions.

It's confusing sometimes.

When I grow up, I guess I will understand more.

That's what some grown-ups tell me.

Right now I'm very busy.

School is almost out.

In a few weeks I'm going to overnight camp.

I know what to bring because I went last year.

So I'm starting to pack my stuff.

And I am learning how to stand on my head.

Good-bye!

GLOSSARY

ADOPT—to become the parents of a child who is already born. People adopt a child because they really want to have a child. When parents adopt a child, they are responsible for taking care of that child. They are the "forever" parents.

BIOLOGICAL PARENTS—the mother and father who give birth to the child. There are many different reasons biological parents can't always take care of their own children, so the child has to be taken care of by other people. If the biological parents can't take care of their child, the courts decide who should take care of that child. Another term for biological parents is "birth parents."

FOSTER FAMILY—a family that takes care of a child when the child's own parents, the biological parents, can't. A foster family is not usually a "forever" family. Often a child will live with one or more foster families before being adopted. A foster family often has more than one foster child at one time.

FOSTER HOME—where a foster family lives. This place can be a house or an apartment. It is called a foster home because foster parents and foster children live there together as a family.

SOCIAL WORKERS—people who help children and grown-ups who have problems. Social workers make sure children are taken good care of. They help find foster parents or adoptive parents when the biological parents cannot take care of their child.

ACKNOWLEDGMENTS

Heartfelt thanks to Jenny, Susan, and R.C. for their ideas, hard work, and good spirit and, most importantly, for sharing their story.

Much appreciation to the following people for their interest and participation in the project: Vivian Banish; Sonya Blackman; Alexa, Gene, Johanna, Layton and Rachel Borkan; Lisa K. Buchanan; Marian E. Collins; Terry Ebert Crawford; Andrew, Jennie and Paul A. Epstein; Paula Fracchia; Sydney Goldstein; Judge Richard Hodge; Nancy Leenheer, DMH; Stephanie, Otis, and Little Otis Morgan; Lois B. Morris; Anita Nathan; Kate Philpott and her fourth graders at San Francisco Day School; Barbara Reid; Neal Sofman; Mrs. Steele and her relay racers at the Chabot School; Wendy Thomas; Marsha Torkelson; Mr. and Mrs. Lung Sang Wong and their gracious extended family; and Robert O. Warren and Catharine Rigby at HarperCollins.

Roslyn Banish

I wrote this book with Roslyn and my family because I wanted to give other people an idea what it's like to be adopted like I was. Not all children had the same experience that I did. This book tells you about me and my family.

I would like to thank
Roslyn Banish
Susan B. Jordan, my mom
Ron Wong, my dad
Jim Carmichael
Nancy Leenheer
These people helped make it possible for this book to be.

Jennifer Jordan-Wong